W9-ABT-016

BEING SAFE WITH FIRE

Bannockburn School Dist. 106
4465 Telegraph Road
Bannockburn, Illinois 60015

BY SUSAN KESSELRING • ILLUSTRATED BY DAN McGEEHAN

The Child's World®

Published by The Child's World®
1980 Lookout Drive • Mankato, MN 56003-1705
800-599-READ • www.childsworld.com

ACKNOWLEDGMENTS
The Child's World®: Mary Berendes, Publishing Director
The Design Lab: Design and production
Red Line Editorial: Editorial direction

LIBRARY OF CONGRESS CATALOGING-IN-PUBLICATION DATA
  Kesselring, Susan.
  Being safe with fire / by Susan Kesselring;
illustrated by Dan McGeehan.
     p. cm.
  Includes bibliographical references and index.
  ISBN 978-1-60954-372-3 (library bound: alk. paper)
  1. Fires—Safety measures—Juvenile literature. 2. Fire prevention—
Juvenile literature. 3. Fire—Juvenile literature. I. McGeehan, Dan, ill.
II. Title.
  TH9148.K47 2011
  628.9'22—dc22   2010040466

Printed in the United States of America
Mankato, MN
December, 2010
PA02069

About the Author

Susan Kesselring loves children, books, nature, and her family. She teaches K-1 students in a progressive charter school down a little country lane in Castle Rock, Minnesota. She is the mother of five daughters and lives in Apple Valley, Minnesota, with her husband, Rob, and a crazy springer spaniel named Lois Lane.

About the Illustrator

Dan McGeehan spent his younger years as an actor, author, playwright, and editor. Now he spends his days drawing, and he is much happier.

How many candles were on your last birthday cake? Do you love to snuggle by a cozy fire? How about roasting gooey marshmallows over a campfire?

Hi! I'm Buzz B. Safe. Watch for me! I'll show you how to be safe with fire.

Fire can be fun and useful. But, as you know, it can also be dangerous. That's why it's so important to learn how to stay safe with fire.

A fireplace or a woodstove can warm you up on a cold winter day. Enjoy the fire, but always stand back a bit. Being too close could burn your skin. Or a stray **spark** could land on your clothes and start a fire.

Matches and **lighters** are adult tools. Let your mom or dad light your birthday candles. If you see matches or lighters lying around, be a helper. Tell an adult right away.

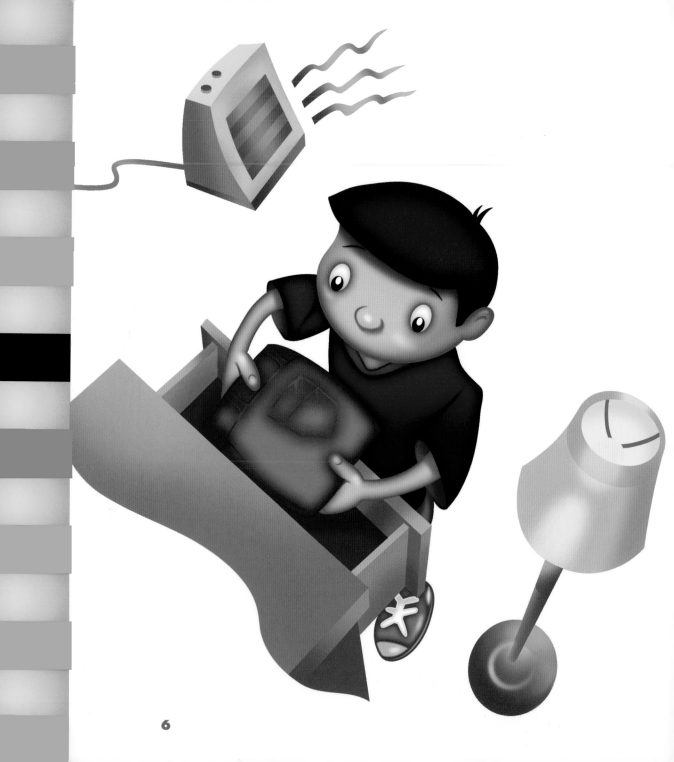

Lamps and heaters can get hot! Store blankets and clothes away from them. These items can catch fire if they touch the hot parts for too long.

Electricity can cause fires, too. Only put plugs into a wall **socket**.

Cooking is fun! You can make dessert for your sister's birthday. To play it safe, always have an adult with you in the kitchen. Hold the handle of the pot while you stir. When you're done, turn the handle toward the back of the stove. If the handle sticks out over the front edge of the stove, it could get bumped. Hot liquid could spill on someone.

Make sure your clothes aren't too loose and you aren't wearing long jewelry. These things could touch the burner and catch on fire.

Smoke detectors can "smell" smoke before people do. Their alarms tell you a fire might be close by. You and your family have time to get outside safely.

Smoke detectors should be on every floor of your home. They should also be in or right outside bedrooms. Smoke detectors need to be placed high on walls— about 4 to 12 inches (10–30 cm) below the ceiling—or on the ceiling. This is because smoke rises.

Don't worry! You might not smell smoke if you are in a deep sleep. But the smoke detector will wake you up.

Fire can move quickly—so you need to act quickly. Knowing what to do beforehand can save your life. With your family, make an escape plan. You should have two ways to get out of each room. Your first choice should be the door. Practice the plan until everyone knows it.

What do you do once you're outside? Go to your family's meeting place. It should be a bit away from the house. Some families meet by the mailbox or a tree. Practice meeting there.

You have fire drills at school, right? Practicing your plan is like a fire drill at home.

If there is a fire, get out of your home as fast as you can. Don't worry about taking anything with you—not a coat or shoes or your favorite book. That wastes precious time.

In a fire, remember to get low and go.

If the smoke is thick, get low to the ground and crawl out. Smoke rises, so the best air will be down near the floor.

If you come to a closed door, carefully feel it with your hands. Start at the bottom and then go up. If it's hot, there may be fire on the other side. Keep the door closed. Find another way to get out.

Firefighters will come to rescue you if you are stuck inside. Don't hide under a bed or in a closet. Stay where they can see you.

If your clothes catch on fire, stay calm. Running could make the fire bigger. Instead, stop, drop, and roll! Stop right where you are. Lie down. Cover your face with your hands. Then, roll back and forth until the fire is out.

Once you are out, stay outside. Going back inside your home is very dangerous. Fire moves quickly, and you could get trapped. No matter what, do not go back inside.

Call 911 on a neighbor's phone. Firefighters will come and put out the fire, and you and your family will be safe.

Firefighters wear special clothes and air tanks to keep them safe in a fire. Do you think they look kind of scary? You don't need to be afraid of them. They are there to help you and your family.

FIRE SAFETY RULES TO REMEMBER

Always be safe!

1. Leave matches, lighters, and candles alone.

2. Don't put anything over a lamp or a heater.

3. Always have an adult help you if you are cooking.

4. Have a plan for getting out of your home in case there is a fire. Practice it until you know it.

5. In a fire, stay low to the ground and get out quickly.

6. If your clothes catch fire, stop, drop, and roll.

7. Never go back into a burning building.

GLOSSARY

lighters (LYT-urs): Lighters are tools used to start a fire. Only adults should use lighters.

smoke detectors (SMOHK di-TEK-turs): Smoke detectors are devices that make loud noises to tell you there is smoke. Smoke detectors can wake you up in time to escape from a fire.

socket (SOK-it): A socket is the place in the wall where you plug in electric cords. Do not put anything other than plugs in a socket.

spark (SPARK): A spark is a small piece of burning material. Stay back from a fire so a spark does not land on your clothes.

TO LEARN MORE

BOOKS
Cuyler, Margery. *Stop, Drop, and Roll*. New York: Simon & Schuster, 2001.

Kalman, Bobbie. *Emergency Workers Are on Their Way!* New York: Crabtree, 2005.

Rau, Dana Meachen. *Fire Safety*. New York: Marshall Cavendish Benchmark, 2009.

WEB SITES
Visit our Web site for links about being safe with fire:
childsworld.com/links

Note to Parents, Teachers, and Librarians: We routinely verify our Web links to make sure they are safe and active sites. So encourage your readers to check them out!